Easy Banana Cookbook

50 Delicious Banana Recipes

By
BookSumo Press

Published by
http://www.booksumo.com

LEGAL NOTES

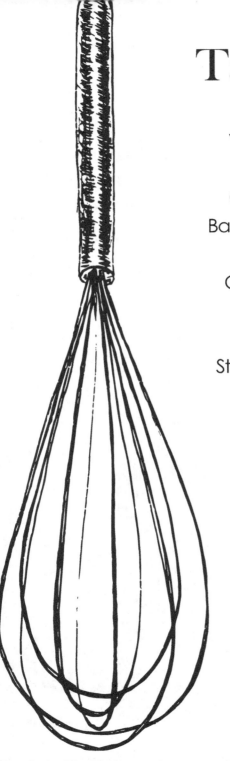

Table of Contents

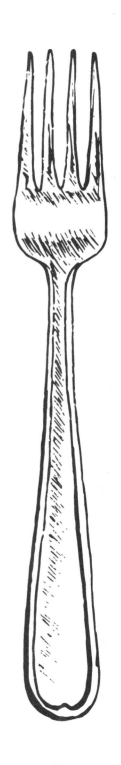

Banana
Fritters

Prep Time: 5 mins
Total Time: 20 mins

Servings per Recipe: 4

Calories	489 kcal
Carbohydrates	73.2 g
Cholesterol	64 mg
Fat	19.5 g
Fiber	5 g
Protein	8.3 g
Sodium	73 mg

Ingredients

1 1/4 cups all-purpose flour
2 tbsps granulated sugar
1/4 tbsp vanilla powder
1/2 cup milk
1 egg
2 tbsps butter, melted
1 tsp rum flavoring

4 ripe bananas, sliced
2 cups oil for frying

Directions

1. Mix flour, vanilla powder and sugar before making a space in the center and adding milk, melted butter, egg and rum flavoring.
2. Combine it thoroughly before adding banana slices.
3. Fry this banana mixture in hot oil for about 15 minutes or until golden brown.
4. Remove these bananas from the oil and drain it well with the help of paper towels.
5. Serve.

CREAM CHEESE
Vanilla Bread

Prep Time: 30 mins
Total Time: 1 hr 15 mins

Servings per Recipe: 16
Calories	289 kcal
Fat	15.1 g
Carbohydrates	35.5g
Protein	4.4 g
Cholesterol	39 mg
Sodium	213 mg

Ingredients

1/2 cup margarine, softened
1 (8 ounce) package cream cheese, softened
1 1/4 cups white sugar
2 eggs
1 cup mashed bananas
1 teaspoon vanilla extract
2 1/4 cups all-purpose flour

1 1/2 teaspoons baking powder
1/2 teaspoon baking soda
3/4 cup chopped pecans
2 tablespoons brown sugar
2 teaspoons ground cinnamon

Directions

1. Coat two bread pans with oil and flour then set your oven to 350 degrees before doing anything else.
2. Get a bowl and begin to stir your cream cheese and margarine until it is completely smooth then combine in the white sugar and continue to stir the mix until it is fluffy.
3. Now combine in the eggs one by one and once all the eggs have been combined in.
4. Add in the vanilla and bananas.
5. Stir the mix again then combine in the baking soda, baking powder, and flour.
6. Work the mix until you have an even and somewhat moist batter.
7. Get a 2nd bowl and combine in the cinnamon, 2 tbsps brown sugar, and the chopped pecans.
8. Pour half of the batter between the bread pan then top each layer of batter with the pecan mix evenly then add in the rest of the batter.
9. Cook everything in the oven for 50 mins.
10. Enjoy.

Banana
& Brown Sugar Spring Rolls

🥣 Prep Time: 10 mins
🕐 Total Time: 20 mins

Servings per Recipe: 8
Calories   325 kcal
Fat   11.6 g
Carbohydrates   53.3g
Protein   3.5 g
Cholesterol   3 mg
Sodium   191 mg

Ingredients

2 large bananas
8 (7 inch square) spring roll wrappers
1 C. brown sugar, or to taste
1 quart oil for deep frying

Directions

1. In a large cast-iron skillet or deep fryer, heat the oil to 375 degrees F.
2. Slice the bananas in half lengthwise and cut into fourths crosswise.
3. Arrange 1 piece of banana over the corner of a spring roll wrapper diagonally and sprinkle with brown sugar.
4. Roll the each corner of the wrapper to the center and fold bottom and top corners in and continue rolling.
5. With your wet fingers brush the edges of the wrapper to seal the roll.
6. Carefully, add the banana rolls in the skillet in batches.
7. Fry the rolls till golden brown and transfer onto paper towel lined plates to drain.

OCTOBER'S
Muffins

Prep Time: 15 mins
Total Time: 35 mins

Servings per Recipe: 10
Calories	263 kcal
Fat	8.1 g
Carbohydrates	46 g
Protein	3.2 g
Cholesterol	38 mg
Sodium	352 mg

Ingredients

1 1/2 cups all-purpose flour
1 teaspoon baking soda
1 teaspoon baking powder
1/2 teaspoon salt
3 bananas, mashed
3/4 cup white sugar
1 egg, lightly beaten

1/3 cup butter, melted
1/3 cup packed brown sugar
2 tablespoons all-purpose flour
1/8 teaspoon ground cinnamon
1 tablespoon butter

Directions

1. Coat ten sections of a muffin tin with oil then set your oven to 375 degrees before doing anything else.
2. Get a bowl, combine: salt, 1.5 cups flour, baking powder, and baking soda.
3. Get a 2nd bowl, combine: melted butter, bananas, egg, and sugar.
4. Now combine both bowls and form a batter.
5. Evenly divide the batter mix between the muffin tin sections.
6. Get a 3rd bowl, combine: cinnamon, 2 tbsps flour, and brown sugar.
7. Add in 1 tbsp of the butter and work the mixture into a crumbly topping.
8. Divide the contents of the third bowl between the muffin tin then place everything in the oven for 22 mins.
9. Enjoy.

Chocolaty Banana
Spring Rolls

🥣 Prep Time: 20 mins
🕐 Total Time: 27 mins

Servings per Recipe: 8
Calories   119.0
Cholesterol   15.9mg
Sodium   47.0mg
Carbohydrates   16.1g
Protein   1.3g

Ingredients

8 large spring roll wrappers
2-oz. unsalted butter, melted
4 small ripe bananas, peeled, sliced lengthwise and
halved diagonally
4-oz. bittersweet chocolate, chopped
Salt, to taste

Directions

1. Set your oven to 425 degrees F before doing anything else and line a baking dish with parchment paper.
2. Arrange 2 wrappers onto a smooth surface and coat with some butter.
3. Arrange one piece of banana over the lower third of the wrapper.
4. Top with chocolate and sprinkle with salt.
5. Fold the inner sides of wrapper around the banana and roll tightly.
6. Repeat with the remaining wrappers and banana pieces.
7. Arrange the rolls on the prepared baking dish in a single layer and coat with the butter.
8. Cook everything in the oven for about 5-7 minutes or till golden brown.

FLUFFY
Banana Pie

🥣 Prep Time: 30 mins
🕐 Total Time: 1 hr

Servings per Recipe: 8

Calories	522 kcal
Fat	25.4 g
Carbohydrates	63.3g
Protein	8.4 g
Cholesterol	115 mg
Sodium	206 mg

Ingredients

1 1/2 cups graham cracker crumbs
1/4 cup butter, melted
2 tablespoons brown sugar
2 (1 ounce) squares bittersweet chocolate
2 tablespoons heavy whipping cream
3 cups low-fat milk
3/4 cup white sugar

2 eggs
1/2 cup all-purpose flour
2 tablespoons apple juice
4 bananas
2 tablespoons lemon juice
1 cup heavy whipping cream
2 tablespoons cranberry juice

Directions

1. Set your oven to 375 degrees before doing anything else.
2. Get a bowl, mix: the brown sugar and butter.
3. Place the mix as a crust in a 10 inch pie dish.
4. Cook the mix in the oven for 12 mins then shut the heat and let everything cool completely.
5. Get a pot of water boiling then place a metal bowl into the pot.
6. Add your chocolate and 2 tbsps of cream to the bowl and begin to melt and stir everything completely.
7. Once everything is melted and combined evenly, shut the heat then place the mix into the pie dish.
8. Let the dish to sit for 20 mins.
9. At the same time begin to heat up your milk just until it begins to simmer then shut the heat.
10. Get a 2nd bowl, combine: flour, eggs, and sugar.
11. Pour in the warm milk gradually and keep stirring then add the mixture to the pot you warmed the

milk in.

12. Get everything boiling while stirring and let it cook for 4 mins.
13. Now shut the heat then add in the cranberry juice and let everything sit for 25 mins.
14. Cut your banana into pieces and place it into a 3rd bowl and mix in the lemon juice.
15. Layer your banana into the pie dish evenly then pour the milk mix over everything.
16. Place everything in the fridge for about 3 hrs.
17. Before serving the dish begin to beat 1 cup of cream until it begins to peak then combine in 2 tbsps of apple juice and beat everything again.
18. Place the mix on top of the pie when serving.
19. Enjoy.

NANA
Cake

🥣 Prep Time: 30 mins
🕐 Total Time: 50 mins

Servings per Recipe: 12
Calories   424 kcal
Fat   13.2 g
Carbohydrates   72.5g
Protein   5.2 g
Cholesterol   77 mg
Sodium   332 mg

Ingredients

3 cups cake flour
1 teaspoon baking powder
1 1/8 teaspoons baking soda
3/4 cup unsalted butter
2 1/4 cups white sugar
3/4 teaspoon salt
3 eggs

1 1/2 cups mashed bananas
6 tablespoons buttermilk
1 teaspoon vanilla extract

Directions

1. Coat three 9" cake pans with oil and flour then set your oven to 375 degrees before doing anything else.
2. Get a bowl and sift in your soda, baking powder, and flour evenly.
3. Get a 2nd bowl, combine: salt, sugar, and butter.
4. Work the mix into an even cream then combine in the eggs one by one.
5. Evenly combine everything completely.
6. Combine the buttermilk, bananas, and flour mix into the cream mix then combine in the vanilla evenly.
7. Enter everything into the cake pans then cook the cakes in the oven for 25 mins.
8. Top the cake with some icing and serve.
9. Enjoy.

Strawberry
& Banana Spring Rolls

Prep Time: 10 mins
Total Time: 20 mins

Servings per Recipe: 4
Calories	60.1
Cholesterol	0.0mg
Sodium	0.8mg
Carbohydrates	15.3g
Protein	0.8g

Ingredients

12 large square rice paper sheets
8 medium strawberries, hulled and sliced
2 bananas, peeled and sliced
7-oz. strawberry flavored vegan soy yogurt
Fresh mint leaves, for garnishing

Directions

1. Soak the rice papers, one by one in a bowl of warm water till soft and transfer onto paper towels.
2. Place the rice papers onto a smooth surface.
3. Divide the strawberry and banana slices in the center of each rice paper evenly.
4. Fold the inner sides of wrappers around the filling and roll tightly.
5. Cut each roll in half and serve with yogurt and a garnishing of mint.

After-School Drink

Prep Time: 5 mins
Total Time: 10 mins

Servings per Recipe: 4
Calories	109 kcal
Fat	1.4 g
Carbohydrates	23g
Protein	2.7 g
Cholesterol	5 mg
Sodium	29 mg

Ingredients

2 bananas
1 cup milk
1/4 cup water
1 kiwi
1 chopped apple
2 tablespoons brown sugar
8 cubes ice

Directions

1. Add your milk and bananas to a blender and add in the brown sugar, and the water.
2. Begin to work the mix into a smoothie then add in the apples, and kiwis and process the mix some more.
3. Now blend in the ice cubes then divide the mix between four serving glasses.
4. Enjoy.

FLUFFY
Pie II

🥣 Prep Time: 30 mins
🕐 Total Time: 1 hr 42 mins

Servings per Recipe: 8
Calories   303 kcal
Fat   11.1 g
Carbohydrates   47.2g
Protein   4.9 g
Cholesterol   89 mg
Sodium   224 mg

Ingredients

3/4 cup white sugar
1/3 cup all-purpose flour
1/4 teaspoon salt
2 cups milk
3 egg yolks, beaten
2 tablespoons butter
1 1/4 teaspoons vanilla extract

1 (9 inch) pie crust, baked
4 bananas, sliced

Directions

1. Add your salt, flour, and sugar to a pan and begin to heat and stir everything.
2. As the mix heats add in the milk and continue to stir everything for 3 mins then shut the heat.
3. Add some of the mix to your yolks in a bowl then combine the yolk mix with the entire flour mix.
4. Continue to heat and stir everything for 3 more mins then shut the heat.
5. Combine in the vanilla and the butter and mix everything in completely.
6. Now cut your banana into pieces then place the pieces on the pie crust add in the flour mix over the bananas and cook everything for 17 mins at 350 degrees in the oven.
7. Enjoy.

Neufchatel
Sandwich

🥣 Prep Time: 15 mins
🕐 Total Time: 15 mins

Servings per Recipe: 8
Calories   289 kcal
Fat   10.3 g
Carbohydrates   40.4g
Protein   10.6 g
Cholesterol   21 mg
Sodium   344 mg

Ingredients

1 (8 oz.) package Neufchatel cheese, softened
1/4 C. crushed pineapple, drained
4 bananas, sliced
1/2 C. shredded coconut
16 slices whole-grain bread

Directions

1. Get a bowl, mix: pineapple and cheese.
2. Coat one piece of bread with this mix and then layer some banana on top of it, top everything with a final layer of coconut.
3. Form a sandwich with another piece of bread.
4. Enjoy.

CREAM CHEESE
Sweet Bars

Prep Time: 30 mins
Total Time: 8 hr 30 mins

Servings per Recipe: 20
Calories	326 kcal
Fat	19.6 g
Carbohydrates	36.4g
Protein	3.3 g
Cholesterol	37 mg
Sodium	155 mg

Ingredients

2 cups graham cracker crumbs
1/2 cup white sugar
1/2 cup butter
16 ounces cream cheese, softened
1 cup white sugar
1 teaspoon vanilla extract
3 bananas, sliced

1 (20 ounce) can crushed pineapple, well drained
1 (12 ounce) container frozen whipped topping, thawed
1/2 cup chopped walnuts
1 (4 ounce) jar maraschino cherries, halved

Directions

1. Set your oven to 350 degrees before doing anything else.
2. Add your butter to a pan then begin to melt it.
3. Once the butter is melted shut the heat and combine in the cracker crumbs and half a cup of sugar.
4. Flatten the crumb mix into a casserole dish then cook it in the oven for 17 mins.
5. Let the crust sit and as it cools combine the vanilla, 1 cup of white sugar, and cream cheese together in a bowl.
6. Top the crust with the cream mix then place your pieces of banana, whipped topping, and pineapple in the crust.
7. Top everything with the nuts then layer on the cherries.
8. Place everything in the fridge for 8 hrs then slice it into servings.
9. Enjoy.

Caribbean
Rice

Prep Time: 15 mins
Total Time: 45 mins

Servings per Recipe: 2
Calories	398 kcal
Carbohydrates	71.6 g
Cholesterol	0 mg
Fat	10.7 g
Fiber	5.6 g
Protein	6.1 g
Sodium	11 mg

Ingredients

1 tbsp vegetable oil
1/2 large onion, sliced
1/2 red apple, cored and sliced
1 pinch curry powder
1 C. water
2/3 C. brown rice
1 tsp dark molasses or treacle

1 small banana, sliced
1 tbsp unsweetened flaked coconut

Directions

1. Get a saucepan. With medium heat, get your oil hot.
2. Stir fry apples and onions until the onions are translucent. Combine your curry and water.
3. Get the water boiling and then mix in rice and molasses. Place a lid on the pan. Set heat to low. Cook for 30 mins.
4. Add banana, and garnish with coconut.
5. Enjoy.

ROLLED OAT
Date Cookies

Prep Time: 15 mins
Total Time: 50 mins

Servings per Recipe: 36
Calories   56 kcal
Fat   2.4 g
Carbohydrates   8.4g
Protein   0.8 g
Cholesterol   0 mg
Sodium   1 mg

Ingredients

3 ripe bananas
2 cups rolled oats
1 cup dates, pitted and chopped
1/3 cup vegetable oil
1 teaspoon vanilla extract

Directions

1. Set your oven to 350 degrees before doing anything else.
2. Get a bowl and crush your bananas in it.
3. Then combine in the vanilla, oats, oil, and dates.
4. Combine everything evenly then let the mix stand on the counter for 20 mins.
5. Layer dollops of the mix on a baking sheet and cook the cookies in the oven for 25 mins.
6. Enjoy.

Chicken
and Rice

🥣 Prep Time: 15 mins
🕐 Total Time: 45 mins

Servings per Recipe: 3	
Calories	916 kcal
Carbohydrates	42.9 g
Cholesterol	113 mg
Fat	61.9 g
Fiber	3.7 g
Protein	34.8 g
Sodium	1322 mg

Ingredients

1/2 C. uncooked long-grain white rice
1 C. water
3 tbsps vegetable oil
1/4 C. butter
3 skinless, boneless chicken breast halves
3 fluid oz. dark rum
1 (6 oz.) can broiled-in-butter-style sliced

mushrooms
2 1/2 tbsps chicken bouillon granules
2 tsps garlic powder
2 tsps ground black pepper
1 (14 oz.) can coconut milk
1 small banana, sliced

Directions

1. Get a saucepan. Bring water and rice to boil. Set heat to low. Let everything cook for 24 mins.
2. Get a frying pan. Heat oil and butter. Stir fry chicken for 7 mins on each side.
3. Cover chicken with rum. Get a match and set the rum on fire (be careful please). Let the flames burn out.
4. Combine in the following: coconut milk, mushrooms, pepper, garlic powder, and bouillon. Set heat to low. Cook for 11 mins.
5. Enjoy chicken and mushrooms with some rice.

CLASSICAL
Oatmeal Cookies

Prep Time: 10 mins
Total Time: 45 mins

Servings per Recipe: 18
Calories	223 kcal
Fat	7.8 g
Carbohydrates	35g
Protein	6.7 g
Cholesterol	0 mg
Sodium	145 mg

Ingredients

1 banana, peeled and mashed
1 cup peanut butter
1/2 cup white sugar
1/2 cup packed brown sugar
2 egg whites
2 cups whole wheat flour
1 teaspoon baking soda

1 cup rolled oats
1 cup raisins

Directions

1. Set your oven to 300 degrees before doing anything else.
2. Get a bowl, combine: brown sugar, bananas, white sugar, and peanut butter.
3. Stir the mix completely then combine in the egg whites.
4. Combine in the baking soda and the flour then add in the raisins and the rolled oats.
5. Layer large dollops of the mix onto a baking sheet and cook the cookies in the oven for 16 mins.
6. Enjoy.

Jamaican Bread II (Banana)

🥣 Prep Time: 45 mins
🕐 Total Time: 1 hr 45 mins

Servings per Recipe: 24
Calories   131 kcal
Fat   3.8 g
Carbohydrates   22g
Protein   1.9 g
Cholesterol   13 mg
Sodium   92 mg

Ingredients

2 tbsps unsalted butter, softened
2 tbsps cream cheese
1 C. white sugar
1 egg
2 C. all-purpose flour
2 tsps baking powder
1/2 tsp baking soda
1/8 tsp salt
1 C. mashed overripe bananas
1/2 C. milk
2 tbsps apple juice
1/2 tsp lime zest

2 tsps lime juice
1 tsp vanilla extract
1/4 C. diced toasted pecans
1/4 C. flaked coconut
Glaze:
1/4 C. brown sugar
2 tsps unsalted butter
2 tsps lime juice
2 tsps grape juice
2 tbsps diced toasted pecans
2 tbsps flaked coconut

Directions

1. Coat 2 bread pans with oil and then set your oven to 375 degrees before doing anything else.
2. Get a bowl and combine your cream and 2 tbsps of butter. Then gradually add in your sugar and mix everything together.
3. Now add in the eggs.
4. Get a 2nd bowl, combine: salt, flour, baking soda, and baking powder.
5. Get a 3rd bowl, mix: vanilla extract, bananas, lime juice, milk, lime zest, and apple juice (2 tbsps).
6. Now combine all three bowls gradually then mix the contents very well for at least 5 mins.
7. Now add 1/4 a C. of the following: coconut flakes and pecans.

8. Evenly divide the mix between your bread pans and cook them for 65 mins in the oven.

9. Get the following gently boiling while stirring: 2 tbsps grape juice, brown sugar, lime juice, and the rest of the butter.

10. Cook this mix for about 2 mins until the sugar is fully incorporated. Shut the heat and add 2 tbsps of coconut and 2 tbsps pecans.

11. Spread the glaze over your bread and then serve.

12. Enjoy.

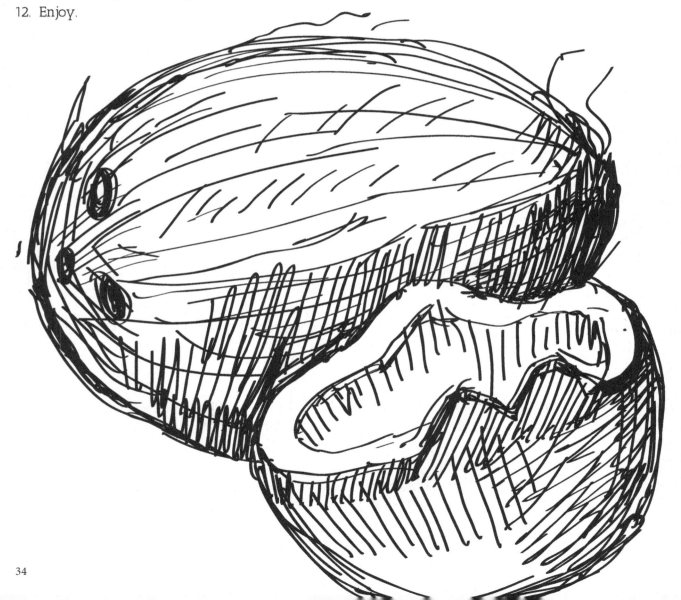

Fruity Brownies

🥄 Prep Time: 15 mins
🕐 Total Time: 45 mins

Servings per Recipe: 16
Calories   151 kcal
Fat   8.2 g
Carbohydrates   19.4g
Protein   1.4 g
Cholesterol   27 mg
Sodium   85 mg

Ingredients

1/2 cup butter
2/3 cup semisweet chocolate chips
1 large egg
2/3 cup packed light brown sugar
1 small ripe banana, mashed
1/2 teaspoon vanilla extract
1/4 teaspoon salt

3/4 cup all-purpose flour

Directions

1. Coat a 9" baking pan with oil then set your oven to 325 degrees before doing anything else.
2. Begin to heat and stir your butter in a pot then combine in the chips and continue to heat and stir everything until the chips are completely melted.
3. Now shut the heat and let everything sit for 10 mins.
4. Get a 2nd bowl and begin to beat your egg in it then combine in the salt, vanilla, banana, and brown sugar.
5. Mix the banana mix with the chocolate mix then combine in the flour and stir everything evenly.
6. Layer the smoothie mix carefully into the baking pan then cook everything in the oven for 35 mins.
7. Enjoy.

BROWN RICE
Jamaican Style

Prep Time: 10 mins
Total Time: 1 hr

Servings per Recipe: 8
Calories   398 kcal
Fat   10.7 g
Carbohydrates   71.6g
Protein   6.1 g
Cholesterol   0 mg
Sodium   11 mg

Ingredients

1 tbsp vegetable oil
1/2 large onion, sliced
1/2 red apple, cored and sliced
1 pinch curry powder
1 C. water
2/3 C. brown rice
1 tsp dark molasses or treacle

1 small banana, sliced
1 tbsp unsweetened flaked coconut

Directions

1. Stir fry your apples and onions in oil until the onions are see-through then add in curry.
2. Cook everything for 1 more min before pouring in your water, molasses, and rice.
3. Get everything boiling before placing a lid on the pot, setting the heat to low, and cooking for 32 mins.
4. Add in the bananas and then your coconuts. Get everything hot again then plate the rice.
5. Enjoy.

Fried
Banana Platter

🥄 Prep Time: 15 mins

🕐 Total Time: 30 mins

Servings per Recipe: 3
Calories	344 kcal
Fat	15.2 g
Carbohydrates	46.1g
Protein	8 g
Cholesterol	131 mg
Sodium	70 mg

Ingredients

1/2 cup all-purpose flour
1 pinch salt
2 tablespoons white sugar
1/4 cup milk
2 eggs
2 large bananas, sliced
2 tablespoons vegetable oil

1/2 tablespoon butter

Directions

1. Get a bowl, combine: the sugar, salt, and flour.
2. Add in your milk slowly and begin to whisk everything to make a batter.
3. Then one by one add in your eggs.
4. Once all the eggs have been added combine in the chopped banana pieces.
5. Get your butter and oil hot then drop dollops of the mix into the pan evenly.
6. Fry the patties until they are browned and crispy then flip each one and continue to fry the opposite side.
7. Top each with some sugar.
8. Enjoy.

HONEY
Walnut Oats

🥣 Prep Time: 5 mins
🕐 Total Time: 7 mins

Servings per Recipe: 1

Calories	532 kcal
Fat	13.1 g
Carbohydrates	101.7g
Protein	11.2 g
Cholesterol	2 mg
Sodium	58 mg

Ingredients

1/4 C. quick cooking oats
1/2 C. skim milk
1 tsp flax seeds
2 tbsps chopped walnuts
3 tbsps honey
1 banana, peeled

Directions

1. For 3 mins microwave: banana, oats, honey, milk, walnuts, and flax. Stir the contents before serving in bowls.
2. Enjoy.

Bed
and Breakfast Pancakes

Prep Time: 10 mins
Total Time: 25 mins

Servings per Recipe: 4
Calories	353 kcal
Fat	10 g
Carbohydrates	58.5g
Protein	7.7 g
Cholesterol	51 mg
Sodium	517 mg

Ingredients

1 egg
2 tablespoons vegetable oil
1 cup milk
1 cup all-purpose flour
1/2 teaspoon baking soda
1/2 teaspoon salt
1/2 cup light brown sugar

1 packet instant, banana-flavored oatmeal

Directions

1. Get a bowl, combine: milk, oil, and egg.
2. Get a 2nd bowl, combine: oatmeal, flour, brown sugar, baking soda, and salt.
3. Combine both bowls evenly then begin to get a skillet hot with oil.
4. Once the oil is hot ladle some of the batter onto the pan and fry one side until it is golden for 4 mins then flip it and continue to fry the opposite side.
5. Enjoy.

ROLLED
Oats and Banana

🥣 Prep Time: 15 mins
🕐 Total Time: 30 mins

Servings per Recipe: 6
Calories	333 kcal
Fat	8.5 g
Carbohydrates	54.7g
Protein	11 g
Cholesterol	38 mg
Sodium	524 mg

Ingredients

1 C. uncooked rolled oats
1 C. whole wheat flour
3/4 C. all-purpose flour
1/4 C. brown sugar
2 tbsps dry milk powder
2 tsps baking powder
1/2 tsp baking soda

1/2 tsp salt
1 egg
2 C. milk
2 tbsps vegetable oil
1 tsp vanilla extract
1 banana, mashed

Directions

1. Blend your oats until powdery.
2. Sift or mix the follow in a bowl: baking soda and powder, oats, salt, regular flour and wheat flour, milk powder, and brown sugar. Place everything to the side.
3. Get a 2nd bowl, mix: beaten eggs, mashed banana, vanilla, and veggie oil.
4. Combine both bowls and let the contents sit for 10 mins.
5. Grease a frying pan and then heat it.
6. Cook large spoonfuls of the mix for about 2 mins per side. Continue for all ingredients.
7. Enjoy with maple syrup.

Quinoa
and Banana

Prep Time: 5 mins
Total Time: 20 mins

Servings per Recipe: 1
Calories	220 kcal
Fat	6.6 g
Carbohydrates	37g
Protein	7.3 g
Cholesterol	1 mg
Sodium	418 mg

Ingredients

1/4 C. water
1/4 C. skim milk
1 tbsp quinoa
1/2 small banana, sliced
1 1/2 tbsps rolled oats
1 tbsp oat bran
1 pinch salt

1 pinch ground cinnamon
1 tbsp chopped walnuts
1 tsp brown sugar
1/4 tsp vanilla extract

Directions

1. Boil: quinoa, milk, and water. Once boiling lower the heat and lightly boil for 6 mins.
2. Add your salt, cinnamon, banana, oat bran, and rolled oats.
3. Stir for 6 mins until everything achieves your desired level of thickness.
4. Turn off the heat and add your vanilla, walnuts, and brown sugar.
5. Enjoy.

BANANA JAM
Topping

Prep Time: 5 mins
Total Time: 15 mins

Servings per Recipe: 12
Calories   77 kcal
Fat   0.3 g
Carbohydrates   20g
Protein   0.8 g
Cholesterol   0 mg
Sodium   1 mg

Ingredients

4 cups mashed ripe bananas
1/3 cup fresh lemon juice
2 tablespoons brown sugar
1/4 teaspoon ground nutmeg

Directions

1. Add your nutmeg, brown sugar, lemon juice, and bananas to the bowl of food processor and puree them.
2. Add the mix to a pan and begin to get it boiling.
3. As the mixture heats stir it slightly until it is thick.
4. Use this as a topping for toasted bread or banana pancakes.
5. Enjoy.

No-Diary
Shake

Prep Time: 5 mins
Total Time: 10 mins

Servings per Recipe: 1
Calories   334 kcal
Fat   12.8 g
Carbohydrates   56g
Protein   3.7 g
Cholesterol   0 mg
Sodium   10 mg

Ingredients

2 bananas, peeled and frozen
1 teaspoon vanilla extract, or more to taste
1/4 cup coconut milk, or more as needed

Directions

1. Add your coconut, vanilla, and banana to the bowl of a food processor and puree the mix into a smoothie.
2. Enjoy.

STIR FRIED
Banana Dessert

🥘 Prep Time: 15 mins
🕐 Total Time: 25 mins

Servings per Recipe: 6
Calories   266 kcal
Fat   12.9 g
Carbohydrates   38.5g
Protein   2.5 g
Cholesterol   15 mg
Sodium   77 mg

Ingredients

3 tablespoons butter
6 ripe bananas, sliced
2 teaspoons vanilla extract
1 cup sweetened flaked coconut
3 1/2 tablespoons confectioners' sugar
1/4 cup chopped walnuts

Directions

1. Get your butter melted in a frying pan then add the chopped banana to the hot butter.
2. Add in the vanilla as well and fry the bananas until they are golden.
3. Add in the coconut and stir everything together then shut the heat and place the bananas and coconut on a serving dish.
4. Garnish everything with some walnuts and the confectioner's.
5. Top some ice cream with this mix.
6. Enjoy.

Stuffed
Dessert Bananas

Prep Time: 10 mins
Total Time: 15 mins

Servings per Recipe: 6
Calories   201 kcal
Fat   5.2 g
Carbohydrates   39.2g
Protein   2.8 g
Cholesterol   3 mg
Sodium   51 mg

Ingredients

6 unpeeled bananas
2 (2.16 ounce) bars chocolate-coated caramel-peanut
nougat candy bars (such as Snickers(R))

Directions

1. Slice out a wedge from the bananas but do not cut it fully then cut each bar of candy into three long pieces.
2. Layer each piece of candy into the banana then place the wedge back on the banana.
3. Cover each banana with some foil then place them in the oven at 300 degrees for 7 mins.
4. Enjoy.

COCOA
Wet Oats

Prep Time: 10 mins

Total Time: 5 m 15 mins

Servings per Recipe: 2
Calories	516 kcal
Fat	9.1 g
Carbohydrates	108.1g
Protein	6.9 g
Cholesterol	0 mg
Sodium	319 mg

Ingredients

2 C. boiling water
1 C. rolled oats
1/4 tsp salt
1/2 C. brown sugar
1 banana, mashed
1/4 C. semisweet chocolate chips

Directions

1. For 6 mins boil your oats in salted water. Turn off the heat and place a lid on the pot. Let the contents sit for about 4 more mins to get thick.
2. Add your chocolate, bananas, and sugar before serving and stir the contents.
3. Enjoy.

Banana
Frozos

🥣 Prep Time: 20 mins
🕐 Total Time: 45 mins

Servings per Recipe: 8
Calories   307 kcal
Fat   16.4 g
Carbohydrates   44.9 g
Protein   3.1 g
Cholesterol   1 mg
Sodium   6 mg

Ingredients

1 (12 ounce) bag chocolate chips
1/4 cup colored candy sprinkles
1/4 cup chopped walnuts
4 bananas, cut in half crosswise

Directions

1. Get a bowl and add in your chips.
2. Place the mix in the microwave for 2 mins then stir them.
3. Get two bowls one for your sprinkles and the other for the nuts.
4. Coat each piece of banana with the chocolate then with the nuts and sprinkles.
5. Cover a baking sheet with some waxed paper then place the bananas on top and put everything in the freezer for 10 mins.
6. Enjoy.

SIMPLY
Sorbet

eat Prep Time: 10 mins
🕐 Total Time: 10 mins

Servings per Recipe: 2
Calories	70 kcal
Fat	0.2 g
Carbohydrates	18g
Protein	0.7 g
Cholesterol	1 mg
Sodium	25 mg

Ingredients

1 frozen banana
1 teaspoon cold water
2 teaspoons caramel sauce

Directions

1. Add your water and banana to a blender then pulse the mix until it chunks. Then combine in the caramel and puree everything completely.
2. Enjoy.

I ♥ Juice

🥣 Prep Time: 10 mins
🕐 Total Time: 10 mins

Servings per Recipe: 2
Calories   320 kcal
Fat   8.9 g
Carbohydrates   53.3g
Protein   11.3 g
Cholesterol   20 mg
Sodium   136 mg

Ingredients

2 cups milk
2 large ripe bananas
2 tablespoons slivered shelled pistachios
1 tablespoon honey

Directions

1. Add your honey, pistachios, bananas, and milk to the bowl of a food processor and puree the mix evenly.
2. Continue to run the processor for 3 mins.
3. Enjoy.

PISTACHIOS
Drink

🥣 Prep Time: 10 mins
🕐 Total Time: 10 mins

Servings per Recipe: 2
Calories	270 kcal
Fat	3.6 g
Carbohydrates	52.1g
Protein	10.7 g
Cholesterol	12 mg
Sodium	126 mg

Ingredients

2 over-ripe bananas, broken into chunks
1 1/4 cups thick plain yogurt
1/3 cup milk, or more to taste
2 ice cubes
2 tablespoons white sugar

Directions

1. Combine your sugar, ice, milk, yogurt, and banana in a food processor and puree the mix completely.
2. Enjoy.

Banana
and Sweet Yogurt

Prep Time: 20 mins
Total Time: 2 h 23 mins

Servings per Recipe: 45
Calories	191 kcal
Fat	0.1 g
Carbohydrates	48.7g
Protein	0.7 g
Cholesterol	0 mg
Sodium	26 mg

Ingredients

6 cups water
4 cups white sugar
5 bananas
1 (46 fluid ounce) can pineapple juice
4 (6 ounce) cans frozen orange juice concentrate
2 (6 ounce) cans frozen lemonade concentrate
2 1/2 (2 liter) bottles lemon-lime flavored carbonated

beverage (such as 7-Up(R))
2 oranges, sliced for garnish

Directions

1. Get your sugar and water boiling in a big pot and let it simmer for 3 mins while stirring.
2. Place the mix in the fridge until it is completely cold.
3. Begin to puree 1 cup of juice and 1 banana in a food processor then continue this process until all the bananas have been added and pureed.
4. Then combine this mix with the cooled syrup completely.
5. Now add your lemon and orange concentrate to the same pot and stir and heat the mix completely.
6. Place the mix into separate pieces of Tupperware and freeze them.
7. Get a big bowl then add in the frozen mix and let it melt until it is slushy then add in the lemon mix and stir everything again.
8. Serve the dish with the orange pieces.
9. Enjoy.

BANANA
Cornbread

Prep Time: 30 mins
Total Time: 1 hr

Servings per Recipe: 24
Calories	197 kcal
Fat	6.8 g
Carbohydrates	31.7g
Protein	2.7 g
Cholesterol	2 mg
Sodium	345 mg

Ingredients

2 cups all-purpose flour
2 cups cornmeal
2 cups milk
2 bananas
1 1/3 cups white sugar
2/3 cup vegetable oil
7 teaspoons baking powder

2 teaspoons salt

Directions

1. Coat a casserole dish with oil then set your oven to 350 degrees before doing anything else.
2. Get a bowl, combine: salt, flour, baking powder, cornmeal, veggie oil, milk, sugar, and bananas.
3. Once the mix is evenly combined and smooth then place everything into the casserole dish.
4. Cook everything in the oven for 35 mins.
5. Enjoy.

Creamy
Salad

🥣 Prep Time: 20 mins
🕐 Total Time: 40 mins

Servings per Recipe: 8
Calories	447 kcal
Fat	32.5 g
Carbohydrates	40.5g
Protein	5 g
Cholesterol	82 mg
Sodium	26 mg

Ingredients

1 pint heavy whipping cream
6 cups seedless red grapes, halved
4 large bananas, peeled and sliced
1 cup chopped walnuts

Directions

1. Get a bowl and whisk your cream until it is peaking then combine in the nuts, grapes, and bananas.
2. Stir everything completely then serve the salad cold.
3. Enjoy.

BANANA
Dump Dessert

Prep Time: 10 mins
Total Time: 2 hr 10 mins

Servings per Recipe: 4
Calories   539 kcal
Fat   20.6 g
Carbohydrates   83.7g
Protein   3 g
Cholesterol   31 mg
Sodium   101 mg

Ingredients

4 bananas, peeled and sliced
4 tablespoons butter, melted
1 cup packed brown sugar
1/4 cup grape juice
1 teaspoon vanilla extract
1/2 teaspoon ground cinnamon
1/4 cup chopped walnuts

1/4 cup shredded coconut

Directions

1. Place your pieces of banana into the crock a slow cooker.
2. Get a bowl, mix: cinnamon, butter, vanilla, grape juice, and brown sugar.
3. Enter this mix over the bananas in the slow cooker.
4. Place a lid on the cooker and let everything cook for 2 hrs with a low level of heat.
5. Then remove the lid and garnish everything with the coconut and walnuts when about 10 mins of cooking time is remaining.
6. Enjoy.

Oven
Bananas and Cloves

🥣 Prep Time: 5 mins
🕐 Total Time: 15 mins

Servings per Recipe: 6
Calories   253 kcal
Fat   11.4 g
Carbohydrates   40.2g
Protein   1.7 g
Cholesterol   20 mg
Sodium   61 mg

Ingredients

1/4 cup butter, softened
1/3 cup brown sugar
1/4 teaspoon ground cloves
1 1/2 teaspoons orange juice
6 bananas, peeled and halved lengthwise
1/3 cup shredded coconut

Directions

1. Coat a casserole dish with oil then set your oven to 375 degrees before doing anything else.
2. Get a bowl, combine sugar and butter.
3. Combine in the orange juice and cloves and work the mix until it is smooth.
4. Layer your bananas in the casserole dish then layer the butter mix evenly.
5. Now layer the coconut over everything and cook the bananas in the oven for 12 mins.
6. Enjoy.

GINGER
Banana Bake

Prep Time: 10 mins
Total Time: 20 mins

Servings per Recipe: 2
Calories   121 kcal
Fat   1.4 g
Carbohydrates   26.3g
Protein   2.6 g
Cholesterol   0 mg
Sodium   293 mg

Ingredients

cooking spray
1/4 cup dry bread crumbs
1 tablespoon granular no-calorie sucralose sweetener
(such as Splenda(R))
1/4 teaspoon ground cinnamon
1/4 teaspoon ground ginger
1 pinch salt

1 large banana, cut into slices

Directions

1. Set your oven to 425 degrees before doing anything else.
2. Get a casserole dish and layer it with some parchment paper.
3. Coat the paper with some non-stick spray.
4. Get a bowl, combine salt, bread crumbs, ginger, sweetener, and cinnamon.
5. Coat your pieces of banana with some more spray then roll the bananas in the cinnamon mix evenly.
6. Place everything in the casserole dish then top the bananas with more spray and layer some more of the cinnamon mix over the bananas.
7. Cook everything in the oven for 12 mins.
8. Enjoy.

Bananas
in San Paulo

🥣 Prep Time: 15 mins
🕐 Total Time: 30 mins

Servings per Recipe: 12
Calories   135 kcal
Fat   3.9 g
Carbohydrates   26.2g
Protein   0.9 g
Cholesterol   5 mg
Sodium   56 mg

Ingredients

6 medium bananas, halved lengthwise
1/2 cup fresh orange juice
1 tablespoon fresh lemon juice
1/2 cup white sugar
1/8 teaspoon salt
2 tablespoons butter
1 cup flaked coconut

Directions

1. Coat a casserole dish with some butter then set your oven to 400 degrees before doing anything else.
2. Layer your bananas in the dish then get a bowl and combine: the salt, orange and lemon juice, and sugar completely.
3. Top your bananas with the wet mix then spread pieces of butter throughout the dish.
4. Cook everything in the oven for 17 mins.
5. Then top the dish with the coconut.
6. Enjoy.

COOKOUT
Bananas

Prep Time: 5 mins
Total Time: 15 mins

Servings per Recipe: 4
Calories	148 kcal
Fat	0.5 g
Carbohydrates	38.1g
Protein	1.5 g
Cholesterol	0 mg
Sodium	3 mg

Ingredients

4 banana, peeled and halved lengthwise
1 tablespoon brown sugar
2 teaspoons lemon juice
2 teaspoons honey
splash of orange juice

Directions

1. Cover a casserole dish with foil then set your oven to 450 degrees before doing anything else.
2. Layer you banana on the dish then top them with the orange juice, brown sugar, honey, and lemon juice.
3. Place a covering of foil on the dish and cook everything in the oven for 7 mins.
4. Enjoy.

Skillet
Buttery Bananas

🥣 Prep Time: 10 mins

🕐 Total Time: 15 mins

Servings per Recipe: 6

Calories	169 kcal
Fat	6 g
Carbohydrates	30.5g
Protein	0.7 g
Cholesterol	15 mg
Sodium	42 mg

Ingredients

3 firm bananas, halved lengthwise
1/2 cup white sugar
1 1/4 teaspoons ground cinnamon
3 tablespoons butter

Directions

1. Slice your banana into two pieces, then cut each half into 4 additional pieces.
2. Get a bowl combine: cinnamon and sugar.
3. Get your butter hot in a frying pan then layer in the banana and fry them for 7 mins.
4. Flip the bananas half way.
5. When serving the bananas coat them with some of the sugar mix.
6. Enjoy

BANANA
Appetizer

🥢 Prep Time: 10 mins
🕐 Total Time: 25 mins

Servings per Recipe: 10
Calories   81 kcal
Fat   4 g
Carbohydrates   8.2g
Protein   3.8 g
Cholesterol   10 mg
Sodium   213 mg

Ingredients

3 bananas, cut into 1/2-inch slices, or more to taste
10 slices turkey bacon, cut in half

Directions

1. Cover each banana with a piece of bacon.
2. Place the bananas in a frying pan and fry them for 20 mins.
3. Roll the banana evenly to fry all sides.
4. Enjoy.

Yellow
Jacket Crepes

Prep Time: 5 mins
Total Time: 20 mins

Servings per Recipe: 6

Calories	518 kcal
Fat	28.7 g
Carbohydrates	60.7g
Protein	8 g
Cholesterol	146 mg
Sodium	252 mg

Ingredients

1 cup all-purpose flour
1/4 cup confectioners' sugar
2 eggs
1 cup milk
3 tablespoons butter, melted
1 teaspoon vanilla extract
1/4 teaspoon salt
1/4 cup butter

1/4 cup packed brown sugar
1/4 teaspoon ground cinnamon
1/4 teaspoon ground nutmeg
1/4 cup half-and-half cream
6 bananas, halved lengthwise
1 1/2 cups whipped heavy cream
1 pinch ground cinnamon

Directions

1. Get a bowl and sift in your powdered sugar and flour. Combine in the salt, eggs, butter, and milk and work the mix completely.
2. Get a frying pan hot with some oil then ladle in about 3 tbsps of the mix and spread the mix to form a nice sized crepe.
3. Let the crepe cook until the bottom is slightly brown for about 3 mins then flip it and cook it the opposite for the same amount of time.
4. When you start another crepe add a bit more oil or butter to the pan.
5. Once all the crepes have been cooked add 1/4 cup of butter to a small pot and get it melted.
6. Combine in 1/4 tsp of cinnamon and nutmeg then add in the brown sugar as well.
7. Stir the mix then stir in the cream and heat everything until it is slightly thick.
8. Begin to fry half of the bananas in the crepe frying pan for 4 mins then top them with the sauce.
9. Place some banana on each crepe then serve it with a topping of more sauce, cinnamon, and whipped cream.
10. Enjoy.

BANANAS
and Fish

Prep Time: 15 mins
Total Time: 45 mins

Servings per Recipe: 6
Calories   246 kcal
Fat   7.1 g
Carbohydrates   17.5g
Protein   24.6 g
Cholesterol   70 mg
Sodium   187 mg

Ingredients

2 tablespoons butter
1 tablespoon all-purpose flour
1 cup milk
6 (4 ounce) fillets sole (or preferred type of fish)
1/2 cup white wine
2 tablespoons fresh lime juice
salt and pepper to taste

3 bananas, sliced lengthwise
1/4 cup grated Parmesan cheese

Directions

1. Set your oven to 350 degrees before doing anything else.
2. Add the following to a pot and begin to heat and stir it completely: milk, flour, and butter.
3. Heat and stir everything until it is completely combined and thick.
4. Layer the sole in a casserole dish then top the fish the sauce then some bananas and the rest of the sauce.
5. Now add a final topping of parmesan and cook everything in the oven for 30 mins.
6. Enjoy.

Colada
Skillet Bananas

🥣 Prep Time: 5 mins
🕐 Total Time: 15 mins

Servings per Recipe: 6
Calories	405 kcal
Fat	19.5 g
Carbohydrates	48.6g
Protein	5.5 g
Cholesterol	23 mg
Sodium	23 mg

Ingredients

1/2 cup semi-sweet chocolate chips
1/3 cup whipping cream
1/2 teaspoon vanilla extract
1/2 cup pina colada soda
1 tablespoon butter
6 bananas, peeled and halved lengthwise
1 cup toasted sliced almonds

Directions

1. Melt and stir the following in a pot: vanilla extract, chocolate and cream.
2. Once the chocolate is completely melted add in the soda and shut the heat.
3. Get your butter hot and melted in a frying pan then combine in the banana and fry them for 4 mins each side.
4. Divide your bananas into servings on plates then top them evenly with the sauce and some almonds.
5. Enjoy.

LEMONY
Banana Chutney

🥣 Prep Time: 10 mins
🕐 Total Time: 35 mins

Servings per Recipe: 1
Calories   145.4
Fat   0.6g
Carbohydrates   0.0mg
Protein   2.2mg
Cholesterol   37.6g
Sodium   1.8g

Ingredients

2 ripe bananas (1 1/2 cups mashed)
2 tablespoons fresh lemon juice
2 pinches ground cloves
1 teaspoon freshly grated lemon rind

Directions

1. With a potato masher or fork, mash the bananas slightly.
2. In a nonreactive bowl, add the mashed bananas and remaining ingredients and bring to a boil.
3. Simmer, stirring occasionally for about 15 minutes or till desired thickness of chutney.
4. Transfer the chutney into hot sterilized jars and seal tightly and refrigerate for a couple of weeks.

ENJOY THE RECIPES?

KEEP ON COOKING
WITH 6 MORE FREE COOKBOOKS!

Click the link below and simply enter your email address to join the club and receive your 6 cookbooks.

http://booksumo.com/magnet

https://www.instagram.com/booksumopress/

https://www.facebook.com/booksumo/

So safe in your arms

is

where

I love to be.

You are a blessing to me.

Daddy,
when you come home
from work
at the end
of the
day

watching you
run
and
explore and play
in the yard

When we all cuddle
at the end of the day